Daily Devotions

31 Days of Joy:

An Eternity of Rejoicing

Ginger L. Ilami

31 Days of Joy: An Eternity of Rejoicing

Cover photo by Ginger L. Ilami

ISBN 978-0615784991

Introduction

This is a 31 day devotional focused specifically on discovering what the Bible has to say about God's joy. Each devotion includes a scripture reading, space to paraphrase and personalize the verse, points to consider, questions for digging deeper, and a closing prayer. I would recommend using a journal along with this book so you will have adequate space to write out your paraphrase and answers to questions. It can be helpful to see how your answers change over time when you go through the devotional more than once. My hope and prayer is and that you will discover God and His joy in a new and powerful way.

- Ginger L. Ilami-

31 Days of Joy

Nehemiah 8:9-10
New International Version 1984 (NIV1984)

[9] Then Nehemiah the governor, Ezra the priest and scribe, and the Levites who were instructing the people said to them all, "This day is sacred to the LORD your God. Do not mourn or weep." For all the people had been weeping as they listened to the words of the Law.
[10] Nehemiah said, "Go and enjoy choice food and sweet drinks, and send some to those who have nothing prepared. This day is sacred to our Lord. Do not grieve, for the joy of the LORD is your strength."

Paraphrase this scripture (put it into your own words and try to include your name as if God were speaking directly to you):

This passage begins with the people hearing the words of the law and weeping. They were convicted of their sin and began to mourn. But Nehemiah tells them to let go of their grief and experience the joy that would give them strength.

We are also convicted of our sin as we read the word of God, and it is appropriate to grieve when we have sinned against our Lord. But it should not stop there. Sorrow over sin is the path that leads us to joy. Conviction points us toward repentance and shows us God's great mercy. Awareness of this mercy and of God's abounding grace toward us will lead us to rejoice. We will find joy when we come face-to-face with the goodness of God in the light of our sin.

Rejoicing in our Lord gives us strength to be obedient and to carry out the tasks God has prepared for us to do. It also gives us a taste of God to help us resist temptation. As you walk through this day, let your grieving over sin be the conduit that leads you to joy in the Lord. This joy will strengthen you for all that God has asked you to accomplish or experience today.

Personal Touch:

Is there sin in your life that you are continuing to grieve over?

If you were to fully turn that over to God and accept His forgiveness, how would your life be different?

Are you missing God's joy in your life? According to this scripture, where do you find God's joy?

Prayer:

"I thank you, Heavenly Father, for your Word and for convicting me of my sins. I confess that I have _(insert any sin needing confession)_ and I thank you for forgiving me and providing for my salvation. I pray that you would fill me with your joy today and that you would turn my weeping into rejoicing over your great mercy and love. Let this joy give me strength to walk the path you have placed before me and avoid any sin that might tempt me. I pray this in the name of Jesus Christ my Savior, Amen."

Psalm 30:10-12
New International Version 1984 (NIV1984)

10 Hear, O LORD, and be merciful to me;
    O LORD, be my help."
11 You turned my wailing into dancing;
    you removed my sackcloth and clothed me with joy,
12 that my heart may sing to you and not be silent.
    O LORD my God, I will give you thanks forever.

Paraphrase this scripture (put it into your own words and try to include your name as if God were speaking directly to you):

This is a prayer of David and an intimate look into how he spoke to God. In this passage he is asking the Lord to hear, be merciful, and be his help in a time of trouble. What a relief to know that we are not the only ones who struggle and suffer in this fallen world. Even the "man after God's own heart" turned to God in prayer asking for mercy and help.

Not only did David ask for mercy and help he also received them. He looks back on a time of great suffering when he was in sackcloth and wailing in his pain. But he recalls God's deliverance that brought him to dancing and wearing his joy like a robe. His heart sang because he could not be silent and he vowed to give God his praise forever – whether God did anything more for him or not.

Never be afraid to ask God for mercy and help. Turn to Him in your suffering with a heart of submission. Never forget the moments where God answered your prayer and delivered you. This is a source of lifelong joy and praise. We never know when the peaks and valleys of our life are going to occur, we only know that they will happen. Remember those "God moments" where He brings you to dancing and clothes you with joy. Do not take them for granted. They can be the nourishment that brings you through the next stormy valley in your life.

Personal Touch:

Describe a time in your past when God answered your prayers and delivered you.

How does remembering this event change your perspective on your current struggles?

How can remembering God's provision and deliverance become a regular part of your life?

Prayer:

"Dear Heavenly Father, thank you for allowing me to come before the throne of grace. I pray for (include a situation that is troubling you) and ask you to have mercy and be a help to me here. I also remember (include a time when God has delivered you) and I praise you for your help and personal touch on my life. Be my guide and help me to always remember the "God moments" you give. May they be a source of strength through future trials. You don't have to be this intimately involved in my life, but you choose to be and I praise you for it. Let my heart never be silent. In Jesus' name I pray, Amen."

Romans 12:11-12
New International Version 1984 (NIV1984)

[11] Never be lacking in zeal, but keep your spiritual fervor, serving the Lord. [12] Be joyful in hope, patient in affliction, faithful in prayer.

Paraphrase this scripture (put it into your own words and try to include your name as if God were speaking directly to you):

In this chapter of Romans, God describes offering our bodies as living sacrifices. God did not place you on this earth, reveal Himself to you as Savior, and begin the work of sanctification so that you could just sit there and look pretty. God's light shines forth from us and it is appealing, but God also calls us to serve Him with zeal and fervor. Getting our eyes off of ourselves and onto God (and those He would have us serve) is key to living a joy-filled life – not a problem-free life, but a joy-filled life.

Our constant source of joy is the hope that we have. What is that hope based upon? Our hope is based in the God of the universe. Not a god who is fickle or changes his mind but a God who is constant, unchanging, stable, totally dependable, and completely loving. Our hope is also in a God who has shared with us how this will turn out in the end. God will triumph over sin and evil and we will spend eternity with Him!

Keeping our focus on God also allows us to manage difficulties of life in a God-centered way. We are to be patient and steadfast as we suffer trials, and we are to remain faithful in prayer. Pray as you cope with life, seek Him, glorify Him for what He is going to bring through your affliction, bask in His glory, have faith in His plan, thank Him for His presence, seek His guidance, and praise Him for blessings.

Our joy can be as dependable as God because it is rooted in the unchangeable God.

Personal Touch:

What things, other than God, have you found yourself putting your hope in and how did that work out?

What does it look like to place your hope in God?

How can you incorporate joy in hope, patience in affliction and faith in prayer into your life today?

Prayer:

"Dear Glorious Father in Heaven, thank you that you are the source of my joy, my patience in affliction and my constant source of strength through prayer. This passage of scripture speaks of serving you by serving others. I pray that you would guide me through (include something that sometimes keeps your eyes away from God) and open my eyes to opportunities where I might bring glory to you by serving others. Give me zeal and fervor in offering myself as a living sacrifice to you. Thank you that you never change and I ask that you would help me to be faithful with the gifts you have given me. In faith and joy I pray, Amen."

Luke 2:9-11
New International Version 1984 (NIV1984)

8 And there were shepherds living out in the fields nearby, keeping watch over their flocks at night. 9 An angel of the Lord appeared to them, and the glory of the Lord shone around them, and they were terrified. 10 But the angel said to them, "Do not be afraid. I bring you good news of great joy that will be for all the people. 11 Today in the town of David a Savior has been born to you; he is Christ the Lord. 12 This will be a sign to you: You will find a baby wrapped in cloths and lying in a manger." 13 Suddenly a great company of the heavenly host appeared with the angel, praising God and saying, 14 "Glory to God in the highest, and on earth peace to men on whom his favor rests."

Paraphrase this scripture (put it into your own words and try to include your name as if God were speaking directly to you):

Here is the classic text that we all know so well. It is easy to skim through this passage because we know the words and most of us have heard them from childhood. But let's take a closer look. First of all, the angel appeared to shepherds. Don't you just love that God so often reveals himself to those the world considers lowly? It is not an earthly measure that God uses when deciding who to enlighten. The angel tells the shepherds that he brings good news of great joy. This news is of great joy! In fact, after the angel tells of the birth of the Messiah, the heavenly host could not hold in their overwhelming joy. Even though one angel could deliver this message, a great company of the heavenly host appeared with the angel bursting forth with joy, giving God all of the glory.

This Messiah was not sent for those who were doing the praising here. The Messiah was sent for man, for you and for me. What God has done here is not just to His glory but to His glory "in the highest". God has made waste of sin and bridged the gap between God and man with the very humiliation of his Son becoming man to die for our salvation. How much more should we rejoice than the heavenly hosts described here. What God has done is for us! His mercy is beyond measure for us! What He has done is not just for those the world deems worthy, it is for all! What joy we should have knowing that the peace God has provided by the sacrifice of His only Son is available to us! Have you forgotten what the Christmas story really means? Find "great joy" in it today!

Personal Touch:

Have you become used to hearing the story of Christmas and how does that impact you?

If the gospel story causes the angels to rejoice, how should you react?

How can you keep the Christmas story as a daily source of joy?

Prayer:

"Dear Heavenly Father, thank you for sending your Son to die for me. Thank you for this scripture showing the rejoicing of the heavenly host. Let it remind me of the import of the news that was shared with the shepherds. Help me to never lose sight of the joy I have in the salvation you have provided. May I not allow (list some distractions) to draw my eyes off of your plans for me here on this earth. Keep my joy fresh every day and let everyone I encounter have an encounter with you. In Jesus' precious name I pray, Amen"

Habakkuk 3:17-19
New International Version 1984 (NIV1984)

[17] Though the fig tree does not bud
and there are no grapes on the vines,
though the olive crop fails
and the fields produce no food,
though there are no sheep in the pen
and no cattle in the stalls,
[18] yet I will rejoice in the LORD,
I will be joyful in God my Savior.
[19] The Sovereign LORD is my strength;
he makes my feet like the feet of a deer,
he enables me to go on the heights.

Paraphrase this scripture (put it into your own words and try to include your name as if God were speaking directly to you):

This passage begins with a list of losses. The prophet is describing the loss of all the necessities, as well as the comforts, of life. Have you ever felt this lost and hopeless? Even though most of us will never experience this level of loss specifically, most of us can relate to this passage on a heart level. The loss of a loved one, families falling apart, a bad diagnosis from the doctor, or feeling utterly alone in an uncaring world. This is the place of no options, no hope.

But, thank our Heavenly Father, the prophet doesn't stop there. Even in the face of such loss he says he will find joy in God. Not only does he rejoice in God his Savior, he also finds strength that enables him to run and achieve. Our joy and rejoicing is firmly planted in the soil that is our God and our salvation. It is natural to fear when faced with potential destruction. It is faith that keeps our eyes on God and allows us to rejoice in the midst of an overwhelming situation.

Turning our difficulties over to God allows us to focus on that which is truly dependable, our Heavenly Father. He never changes in an increasingly unstable world. It is then that we gain strength to run the race placed before us, and then that we can achieve the heights God desires for us. Turn it all over to God and find joy and strength in His presence.

Personal Touch:

What are you currently facing that might draw your focus away from God?

How might your life be renewed if you looked to God, rather than yourself or someone else, as your stability, strength, and joy?

How can you work toward that goal today?

Prayer:

"Dear Heavenly Father, I come before you humble and thankful that you care about me and my situation. I am fearful about (insert something from your life). Life is hard but I know that I can place my trust in you to be my joy and strength no matter how chaotic and frightening my world becomes. Father, keep my eyes firmly on you so that my feet can run like a deer and that I might achieve the heights you desire for me. In Christ my Savior I pray, Amen"

Psalm 145:6-8
New International Version 1984 (NIV1984)

6 They will tell of the power of your awesome works,
and I will proclaim your great deeds.
7 They will celebrate your abundant goodness
and joyfully sing of your righteousness.
8 The LORD is gracious and compassionate,
slow to anger and rich in love.

Paraphrase this scripture (put it into your own words and try to include your name as if God were speaking directly to you):

There is no end to what God has done. Everywhere we look we see His works. In our lives God has accomplished deeds greater than we can imagine. The very nature of God is awesome to contemplate and ever so revealing. He is worthy of never ending praise.

God is goodness. God is <u>abundant</u> goodness. The storehouses of God's goodness will never be empty. The celebration of God's great goodness will be endless throughout eternity. But He is also righteous and perfect justice. As we rejoice in God's goodness we must also joyfully sing of His righteousness. Only our Sovereign Lord could provide a plan that meets the requirements of both His goodness and His justice. We need only believe and partake.

The praise continues because God is also gracious and compassionate. His grace provides us with salvation and power with which to live. He is also compassionate to those in need and slow to anger toward those who offend. Over all of this, God is rich in love. God does not save us and leave us. He showers us with His power, goodness, righteousness, grace, compassion, patience and love. Oh, what a Heavenly Father we have!!

Don't let your days go by with a flippant attitude toward your Heavenly Father, who He is, and what He has done for you. Tell of His works, proclaim His deeds, celebrate His goodness, joyfully sing of His righteousness, and bask in His grace, compassion, patience and love.

Personal Touch:

Describe evidence of God's goodness in your life.

Describe evidence of God's compassion and grace at work in your life.

How can you spend today celebrating your Heavenly Father?

Prayer:

"Dear Heavenly Father, I am undone by your nature and your deeds. Who am I to have such a personal, intimate relationship with the Creator of the Universe? I sing joyfully of your goodness and mercy that will never run out or lessen in any way. I celebrate your grace and compassion that carries me when I can go no farther. I praise you for (include something specific about God's nature that moves you). Help me to never forget to worship you. Make my life a joyful song that others will hear and respond to. In Jesus' precious name I pray, Amen."

James 1:2-3
New International Version 1984 (NIV1984)

[2] Consider it pure joy, my brothers, whenever you face trials of many kinds, [3] because you know that the testing of your faith develops perseverance.

Paraphrase this scripture (put it into your own words and try to include your name as if God were speaking directly to you):

It is fascinating how often verses about joy are also about suffering. The two are often intertwined, and we can't live the fantasy that joy is a solitary experience. We will all face trials. The Bible is very clear that Christians will suffer. This passage in particular does not use the word "if" we face trials but "whenever" we face trials. The trials are even described as "trials of many kinds". The devil seeks to use trials to bring about the downfall of Christians - but God, who is ultimately in control of what is allowed in our lives, has a different purpose for these events. He desires that such formidable situations will be the catalyst for spiritual growth, joy and intimacy with Him.

The pure joy described here comes from the knowledge that the testing of your faith through trials can bring about perseverance, endurance, steadfastness and loyalty. But why would that bring about rejoicing? Ultimately, it is because God wants a closer and more personal relationship with you. Have you ever noticed that nothing creates intimacy faster and more deeply than going through something very difficult with someone? God yearns for you to experience closeness with Him that you have never had with anyone else. Knowing that God can use your trials to deepen your relationship with Him and make you stronger for future experiences is how joy blossoms through the foulness of life. When you feel like you're sinking in the mire, remind yourself that God wants to use this experience to personally walk with you and guide you to a place of unwavering intimacy and faith in Him.

What joy to know that God, who needs nothing from us, desires to be this close and involved with us!

Personal Touch:

What trials are you dealing with right now?

What might happen if you change your thinking about this trial and consider it pure joy because of God's ultimate plan?

How can your struggles deepen your relationship with God today?

Prayer:

"Dear Heavenly Father, thank you for the trials that you are using in my life to draw me closer to you. I pray that you will use (describe a current trial) to increase my faith in you, strengthen my walk with you, and deepen my relationship with you. Help me to seek you as I submit to this experience. I can't wait to see what you are going to do with my life to bring about your glory. I consider it pure joy knowing that you are with me and desiring increased intimacy with me. In the name of my Savior, Jesus, I pray, amen."

John 16:24
New International Version 1984 (NIV1984)

24 Until now you have not asked for anything in my name. Ask and you will receive, and your joy will be complete.

Paraphrase this scripture (put it into your own words and try to include your name as if God were speaking directly to you):

Prayer is a necessary part of the Christian life. This is part of our means of communication with God, and we are commanded to fellowship in this way. Prayer is a sweet, precious means of bringing our life into increasingly intimate contact with all parts of the trilogy - Father, Son and Holy Spirit. This passage speaks of praying in Jesus' name. The focus is on our complete unworthiness and the complete worthiness of Jesus Christ.

In His sacrifice of himself on our behalf He has bridged the gap between God and man, and allows us to come before the throne of grace in prayer. We are to pray in a position of complete submission to the power and plan of the Father. When we pray with complete submission to the will of God and in the name of Christ we will receive answers. It won't always look like what we expect but it will be within the will of God. When we ask and receive in this position of obedience we will have joy that is complete, full, with no room for more.

Does your prayer life look like this? Does it bring about a joy that is complete and full to the brim? Consider the privilege we have in being allowed to communicate personally with the God of the Universe. Come before the Father with a sense of the sacrifice that was required to save us, and submit to the will God has for your life. The experience will be a personal, intimate interaction with our Creator that fulfills the plans of God in our world. Experience God in this way and be prepared to have complete joy!!

Personal Touch:

What might be lacking in your prayer life?

What does it mean to pray with complete submission?

How can you improve your prayer life today?

Prayer:

"Dear Heavenly Father, I come before you humbled and completely grateful for what Christ has done for me. Thank you that I can come before your throne of grace. Help me to submit to (include an area of struggle in your life) and be obedient to your word. I thank you that you are in control and that you have a plan for my life. Guide me in every decision and help me to bring glory to you with all that I do and say. Thank you in advance for what I will receive and I anticipate experiencing your complete and overflowing joy. In Jesus' Holy name I pray, Amen."

Psalm 90:13-14
New International Version 1984 (NIV1984)

¹³ Relent, O LORD! How long will it be?
Have compassion on your servants.
¹⁴ Satisfy us in the morning with your unfailing love,
that we may sing for joy and be glad all our days.

Paraphrase this scripture (put it into your own words and try to include your name as if God were speaking directly to you):

This verse is a part of a prayer written by Moses after Israel rebelled in the wilderness. God passed the sentence that they would wander in the wilderness instead of going straight to the Promised Land. In this prayer, Moses describes the vastness of God and the smallness of humanity. There is confession of sin and a plea for wisdom. Then he asks God to relent and have compassion on them. He pleads not on the basis of their own merit but on the merit of God and His great mercy – that God's mercy and compassion would be a source of future joy and happiness in the wake of their sinfulness.

Have you found yourself wandering in a wilderness? Even though there is often consequence to sin, God does not leave us alone. Confess, repent and turn away from sin in your life. God is compassionate and merciful. He will satisfy you in the morning with His unfailing love. We all sin against God but He provides this way back to fellowship with Him so that we can sing for joy and be glad all our days.

God wants to restore you and bring you back to a place of joy and happiness in Him. He is bigger than your sin no matter what it might be. His provision is enough. Confess and turn away from sin knowing that He has washed you clean. Then you will sing for joy and be glad all your days.

Personal Touch:

Is there anything that might be impeding your fellowship with God?

After confessing your sins do you struggle with forgiving yourself and living within the grace of God?

What can you do today to turn from your sin, accept God's forgiveness, and enjoy the joy God has to offer?

Prayer:

"Dear Heavenly Father, I come before you confessing that I am a sinner. I confess (include any sin needing confessing) and thank you for your forgiveness through the sacrifice of your Son. I pray that you would help me to be obedient and to turn from this sin in the future. Help me be the person you desire me to be so that I might be useful to you. Bring me back to a place of joy and gladness because of your great mercy and unfailing love. May I be humble but wise and may I sing for joy and be glad all my days. In Jesus' name I pray, Amen."

Galatians 5:22-23
New International Version 1984 (NIV1984)

²² But the fruit of the Spirit is love, joy, peace, patience, kindness, goodness, faithfulness, ²³ gentleness and self-control. Against such things there is no law.

Paraphrase this scripture (put it into your own words and try to include your name as if God were speaking directly to you):

For believers, this list of the fruit of the Spirit is a description of our renewed nature. Death to sin leads to life in Christ. The Spirit residing within us brings forth this new nature. Submission to the power of the Spirit allows the light of this new nature to shine forth, with the purpose of others seeing it and glorifying our Father in heaven. Who can see this list and not desire this in their life? First we must unclench our grip on our sinful desires. In Galatians 5, God tells us that we have the freedom to choose sin or life by the Spirit, but we cannot have both. We still have the Spirit and the new nature within us, but choosing sin closes the door on both.

The second item on this beautiful list is "joy". I don't know about you, but I desire this celebration in my life. Once again, we discover that this joy doesn't come from ourselves but rather from God. Submission to living by the Spirit opens the door to release this new nature that resides within us. With the freedom we have been given we can choose Christ rather than sin. How blessed to know that having joy and the rest of the "fruit" in our life is not dependent on our own abilities but on the bedrock foundation of our Heavenly Father. When we let go and submit to God, the Spirit produces this fruit for us and it is based upon Him, not on us or our circumstances.

Is the sin that you are grasping worth giving up love, joy, peace, patience, kindness, goodness, faithfulness, gentleness and self-control?

Personal Touch:

What do you need to let go of in order to grab hold of the life God promises?

How can you choose God rather than sin today?

What would your life look like if you chose to live under the power of the Holy Spirit more often?

Prayer:

"Dear Heavenly Father, I am so blessed to have a God that desires me to embody love, joy, peace, patience, kindness, goodness, faithfulness, gentleness and self-control. Lord, I come before you grateful for this new nature that is available to me, a sinner. Lord, reveal to me any sins that I am grasping onto, anything that is coming between you and me. I come before you confessing (<u>list known sins, especially those you tend to cling onto</u>). In the freedom I have in Christ I choose to submit to you, Father, and I pray that your Holy Spirit would be free to work in me and that His fruit would shine forth through me. Let this light bring glory to you and you alone. In Jesus' name I pray, Amen."

Philippians 2:1-2
New International Version 1984 (NIV1984)

[1] If you have any encouragement from being united with Christ, if any comfort from his love, if any fellowship with the Spirit, if any tenderness and compassion, [2] then make my joy complete by being like-minded, having the same love, being one in spirit and purpose.

Paraphrase this scripture (put it into your own words and try to include your name as if God were speaking directly to you):

Christ died to pay the price for our sins. He sacrificed himself to save us. We are united with Christ and belong to Him. We have the Holy Spirit living within us to guide and help us. This is love beyond all measure! Have you enjoyed any encouragement, comfort, fellowship, tenderness or compassion from your relationship with your Savior? There is nothing that compares to being loved by someone who is sovereign, who knows everything you have done or ever will do and who loves you anyway. This is a love found nowhere else in this world!!

What do we do with this love? Paul tells the Philippians that it would make his joy complete to see them take what they have experienced with God and share it with others. We are to take this inexplicable love and turn it toward others by being like-minded, loving, sharing the same spirit and purpose. God's love is not a love to be gathered in and kept just for ourselves. This is a love that is meant for others. There is great joy when our spiritual leaders see us sharing our experience of God with others, but there may be greater joy for us in opening our hearts and allowing God to flow forth.

Personal Touch:

What encouragement or comfort have you experienced from your relationship with Christ?

How do you share that experience with others?

How can you be more deliberate in sharing what God has given you with others?

Prayer:

"Dear Heavenly Father, I praise you for being such a giving, tender and compassionate Father. You do not have to have this kind of relationship with me but you choose it anyway. You sought me out. Thank you for your encouragement, comfort, and fellowship. I could not walk this path without you. Please help me to open myself up and share my experiences with others. Give me your joy through being one in spirit and purpose with you and with others. In the name of Christ I pray, Amen"

Isaiah 49:13
New International Version 1984 (NIV1984)

¹³ Shout for joy, O heavens;
rejoice, O earth;
burst into song, O mountains!
For the LORD comforts his people
and will have compassion on his afflicted ones.

Paraphrase this scripture (put it into your own words and try to include your name as if God were speaking directly to you):

Oh, to hear the heavens, the earth and the mountains burst into songs of rejoicing! What a time of worship! The very creation is experiencing the joy that is found in God our Savior. The earth is under the curse of sin and, therefore, looks forward to the redemptive work of Christ and rejoices.

Creation finds joy in God's provision of salvation and the care He provides along the way. Our Lord does more than just save us. He could have provided salvation and then left us to struggle through life on our own but He didn't. There is joy in knowing that God comforts his people. He loves us deeply and does not leave us or forsake us. His desire is for us to seek Him and allow Him to provide us with comfort and compassion as we struggle through life in a fallen world. Will you join in the singing? Will you burst into song? You can because God can save you and will give you comfort – comfort provided by the Creator of the universe. Now there is a source of joy!!

Personal Touch:

How does God's work in creation add to your worship experience?

How has God provided comfort and compassion as you struggle through life?

What does it look like when we live a life of worship and joy?

Prayer:

"Dear Heavenly Father, thank you for creating such beauty in our world. Thank you for showing me a little part of yourself in the heavens, the earth and the mountains. But it is easy to lose sight of you as I walk through (list something that is afflicting you at this time). I will take joy, however, in your salvation and the care and comfort you provide every day. Help me not to lose sight of the compassion you give me every day. Help me to recognize the comfort you give and feel your presence with me. Open my eyes that I may rejoice and burst into songs of praise as I behold your faithful compassion for me. In Jesus' name I pray, Amen."

Luke 15:4-6
New International Version 1984 (NIV1984)

[4] "Suppose one of you has a hundred sheep and loses one of them. Does he not leave the ninety-nine in the open country and go after the lost sheep until he finds it? [5] And when he finds it, he joyfully puts it on his shoulders [6] and goes home. Then he calls his friends and neighbors together and says, 'Rejoice with me; I have found my lost sheep.'"

Paraphrase this scripture (put it into your own words and try to include your name as if God were speaking directly to you):

All believers were lost sheep before they were found by their Shepherd. This lost sheep is wandering around in unbelief experiencing the terrors of life without the protection of the Shepherd. Our Savior sought after us and found us. We were weary and fearful but Christ joyfully put us on His shoulders and carried us where we could not go on our own.

Have you ever thought about your Savior searching for and then rejoicing over you? We are sinners of the worst sort. All fall short of the glory of God. Yet He pursued us until He found us. He joyfully placed us on His shoulders and carried us home. Then He called others to rejoice with Him over our salvation. This is a care and concern that we do not, to be perfectly honest, deserve.

So what do you do with this parable of the care and joy of our Savior? Praise God for His pursuit of you in your sinfulness, rejoice in the personal relationship you have with God, rest in His arms when He carries you, and have peace knowing that the Savior is Sovereign and may be pursuing one of your loved ones at this moment.

Personal Touch:

How does it change you to know that your Heavenly Father pursued you?

What does it look like to rest in God's arms?

How is God being a shepherd in your life currently?

Prayer:

"Dear Heavenly Father, thank you for seeking after me when I was still a sinner. Thank you for saving me and carrying me on your shoulders when I was weary. I am humbled that you care so deeply for me. Help me to never take that for granted. Now that I am yours, be my guide in every decision and help me to be worthy of my calling. I know that I can't do this under my own power so please let your joy oil the wheels of my obedience so that I might live under the power of the Holy Spirit. May I never forget what you have done for me. In Jesus' name I pray, Amen."

Psalm 126:5
New International Version 1984 (NIV1984)

[5] Those who sow in tears
   will reap with songs of joy.

Paraphrase this scripture (put it into your own words and try to include your name as if God were speaking directly to you):

I have cried many a tear in my day, and this verse is a source of hope in the times of great pain. This passage speaks to those in captivity. They are people who sow in tears. There is grief and suffering but these captives decide to continue to sow for God, even if in tears. They do so with the expectation of a harvest. Even when we weep, God is to be the focus of our world. Cry out to God, confess any sin, and submit to the plans of the Sovereign. God will use even our tears to bring about His plan.

Weeping with God in mind is not our usual approach to grieving. Usually, weeping is very self-focused. Instead, give it all to God in your tears. Give Him your anguish, self-pity, hopelessness, anger, bitterness, lack of trust and sinfulness. Lay it all out. He already knows. He can take it. When we sow tears at the feet of our King we can expect a harvest of songs of joy. Our tears may be for ourselves or for others, but God can use them to bring rejoicing – now or in eternity.

What is holding you captive? Whether it is a painful diagnosis, family struggles, a seemingly hopeless situation, sin, consequences of sin, whatever it may be, sow your tears at the feet of your Savior. Let it all go to Him. He will use you to take part in His glory if you let Him. God knew the number of your days before you were born. He knows the plans He has for you now. Waiting is tough, but rest in your Father's arms. We can rejoice that God will not let our tears go to waste even if we can't see the ultimate plan. Our time in this world will seem but a moment compared to an eternity of songs of joy with Him.

Personal Touch:

Describe a time when you were grieving.

Is there anything that might be holding you captive now?

What would it look like if you sowed your tears for God? What would you harvest?

Prayer:

"Dear Heavenly Father, I bring my tears to you. I place (include whatever situation is grieving you) into your capable hands. I even give you (include whatever your feelings might be about this situation). Help me to trust in you and the plan you have for my life even when I don't understand. Thank you that you care about every tear I shed. Help me to sow my tears for your glory that they might not go to waste. May they be seeds that grow into a great harvest of rejoicing. In Jesus' name I pray, Amen."

Colossians 1:10-12
New International Version 1984 (NIV1984)

[10] And we pray this in order that you may live a life worthy of the Lord and may please him in every way: bearing fruit in every good work, growing in the knowledge of God, [11] being strengthened with all power according to his glorious might so that you may have great endurance and patience, and joyfully [12] giving thanks to the Father, who has qualified you to share in the inheritance of the saints in the kingdom of light.

Paraphrase this scripture (put it into your own words and try to include your name as if God were speaking directly to you):

The grace of God is larger than life. He has taken sinners who deserve hell and reconciled them (through the death and resurrection of his Son) to himself. As a believer, you now share in the inheritance of the saints in the kingdom of light. What joy that thought should bring forth in your very soul!!

The joy of salvation demands action and change in how we live our lives. The grace of God is a force in our lives and gives us strength to live a life worthy of our Lord. God is mighty and makes His power available to us so that we can have endurance, patience and joy. Just think! God Almighty is willing to not only save us but willing to share his power with us so that we can live the life He desires. God has not asked us to do something without making His power available for the task. In that power is also joy.

It is time to have a new view of your life. Look at your life through the filter of Christ and through the filter of eternity. God is not hiding from you. He desires that you find Him and if you seek Him you will find Him. When you find Him He will empower you to live that worthy life. In that process is true joy! Will you take one step today toward that glorious might?

Personal Touch:

How has your life changed because you share in the inheritance of the saints in the kingdom of light?

Have you been able to tap into the endurance, patience, and joy that God makes available to you? If not, what is preventing you?

How can you seek God today and take part in the power of God's grace?

Prayer:

"Dear Heavenly Father, I thank you for making your glorious might available to me so that I can be strengthened with all power. I also thank you that I am qualified to share in the inheritance of the saints in the kingdom of light simply by believing that your son, Jesus Christ, died on the cross to pay the penalty for my sins and that he rose again so that I can spend eternity with you. I thank you that every day I can access your power to bear fruit, endure with patience, and joyfully experience the life you desire for me. Father, please help me in the area of (include an area of your life where you struggle living worthy of the Lord). I give this part of my life to you and ask that you would empower me to take my eyes off of myself and focus solely on you. Give me your guidance as I seek you with my whole heart. In Jesus' holy name I pray, Amen."

John 16:22
New International Version 1984 (NIV1984)

²² So with you: Now is your time of grief, but I will see you again and you will rejoice, and no one will take away your joy.

Paraphrase this scripture (put it into your own words and try to include your name as if God were speaking directly to you):

What grief the followers of Christ experienced when He was crucified. To have walked with God, sat at His feet, learned from His words and actions, and then to suddenly be without Him must have been devastating. Grief and sorrow is the lot of those without the presence of Christ. When He returned after the resurrection, He gave them the joy of His presence that no one would ever be able to remove.

The world will try to take away your joy. The world tried to remove Christ permanently by crucifying Him. The enemy is always working to separate you from the love of God. Joy stealers want to bring everyone down into the pit where they live. These pits are well appointed and decorated to the nines but they are still just a pit. The presence of Christ is our joy, and no one can remove that unless we let them.

As believers, we have the presence of Christ but we do not always practice the presence of Christ. We can, in effect, close the door on Christ and attempt to get through life with Him in a separate place in our heart. When we close the door on Christ, we also close the door on His joy. This is like living in a black and white world rather than in the brilliant color that God desires for us.

Bask in the presence of Christ today so that you will experience His unending joy. No matter the situation, keep your eyes on Christ and know that joy is available to get you through anything.

Personal Touch:

How have you experienced the presence of God in your life?

Have you ever had someone or something attempt to steal your joy? Have you ever given it away?

How can you practice the presence of Christ today?

Prayer:

"Dear Heavenly Father, thank you for your unending joy. Thank you for the presence of Christ in my life. Sometimes it is difficult and I lose your joy. Please help me with (include something or someone that inhibits your joy). Help me to recognize the joy stealers in my life and help me to keep the door opened to your presence. Thank you for giving me access to rejoicing that will go on into eternity. In Jesus' precious name I pray, Amen."

Psalm 119:111-112
New International Version 1984 (NIV1984)

[111] Your statutes are my heritage forever;
  they are the joy of my heart.
[112] My heart is set on keeping your decrees
  to the very end.

Paraphrase this scripture (put it into your own words and try to include your name as if God were speaking directly to you):

Laws, rules, and statutes are not necessarily what we think of when we picture joy and rejoicing. Most of us desire a time when we will be free of the rules and regulations of a parent, a teacher, a boss. God, however, has given us His word to show us the way we should live this life He gave and designed for us. This is not to say that if we keep all of God's statutes we will live the perfect life and never experience suffering. God's word is our guide and a help as we go through the sanctification process that is life. This process is often painful, but when we keep God as our focus and steep ourselves in His word and His promises, it is then that we are free to experience the joy He desires for us. To read God's word is to be in the very presence of God and to know the mind of God.

The Bible tells us that Jesus Christ is "The Word". Jesus is present in the very words in your Bible. The unspeakable joy that comes from communing with your Savior comes through finding the intimacy of the truth of His promises. God's word is truth – the only truth we can rely on completely. Allow this truth to soak into your inner being. The joy found there is not superficial; it goes deep within your heart and can be your heritage forever.

This joy can only be found in action. Rejoicing comes from making God's Word a priority in your life. Daily reading, meditation, memorization, and application to your day-to-day life are required. God has given you a beautiful gift, but you have to open it and put it on. It is then that you will be clothed in joy. What will you wear today?

Personal Touch:

How does obedience to God's word bring freedom and joy?

What might that look like in your life?

How can you make God's word more of a priority in your life today?

Prayer:

"Dear Heavenly Father, I thank you for giving me your words to guide and cover me. Thank you for Jesus, who is "The Word". I pray that you will help me to be obedient in reading, meditation, memorizing, and applying your word to my life. Guide me and help me not allow (list what prevents you from spending time in God's Word) to be a barrier between you and me. Let your statutes be the joy of my life, and may they clothe me with your very presence. May my heart be set on keeping your decrees to the very end. In Jesus' name I pray, Amen."

Philippians 1:3-5
New International Version 1984 (NIV1984)

³ I thank my God every time I remember you. ⁴ In all my prayers for all of you, I always pray with joy ⁵ because of your partnership in the gospel from the first day until now,

Paraphrase this scripture (put it into your own words and try to include your name as if God were speaking directly to you):

What does your prayer life look like? Is it so fulfilling that you seek it, desire it, or miss it? Prayer was very important to the Apostle Paul, and here he uses the words "my God" when describing how he spoke to the Father. Do you pray like this? You should. God desires this kind of personal and intimate relationship with you. Christ died and rose again so that the veil could be torn and you could have access to the throne of grace. His sacrifice was enough and He wants to be your God! To hold Him at arm's length is to miss out on the deeply personal connection He seeks to have with you.

Paul also describes his deep connection with the Philippians because of their common bond of the gospel. Friendship with a fellow believer is a connection made in heaven. There is nothing like having someone to walk the path of suffering and trials (which we are told to expect) along with us. There is nothing that can replace having a friend who speaks truth and who will help hold up the shield of faith when the devil's arrows are flying. If you don't have such friends, seek them through fellowship and Bible study opportunities in your local church, and especially through prayer. Do you have friendships that you have neglected? We all get busy, but don't disregard those people God has placed in your life. Praise God for them with joy.

God is seeking a deep relationship with you. Allow the blessings God places in your life to draw you close to Him. Pray with joy to your God and praise Him for the friends and partners He gives you for the journey.

Personal Touch:

Describe your current prayer life.

How might you change your prayer life to help it become more personal, intimate, and joyful?

How can you reach out to others, simply for the Glory of God, today? Remember that this doesn't always have to involve a great deal of time.

Prayer:

"Dear Heavenly Father, thank you for being mine. Thank you for choosing me. I praise you for my friendships with (include names of friends and family). They are a blessing to my life and help me as I seek to walk your path. May the blessings you have given me ultimately bring glory to you. I pray with joy for (include a friend needing prayer) and I ask that you would meet his/her needs according to your will. Thank you, Father, for the joy of my partners in Christ and I ask that where I lack in this area you would provide. In Jesus' name I pray, Amen."

Luke 6:22-23
New International Version 1984 (NIV1984)

[22] Blessed are you when men hate you, when they exclude you and insult you and reject your name as evil, because of the Son of Man. [23] "Rejoice in that day and leap for joy, because great is your reward in heaven. For that is how their fathers treated the prophets.

Paraphrase this scripture (put it into your own words and try to include your name as if God were speaking directly to you):

Rejection and persecution are rarely sources of joy in our lives. But here we are told that when we face such pain because of our living for Christ we should, in fact, rejoice. Many songs, stories and poetry have been written about rejection. Most of us would never return to high school because of the rejection and isolation we faced there. The world does not like seeing the darkness of its existence revealed by the light of Christ within us.

We have all faced rejection and exclusion in our lives, but have you faced being called "evil" for the sake of the Christ? This is a whole new game. To be persecuted for your belief and especially for living your belief is often a most hurtful and tragic circumstance. Jesus tells us in this passage that we are not alone, and we are in fact in good company.

When these times come, and you feel hurt and rejected, rejoice and leap for joy. Your joy, once again, comes from keeping your focus on the eternal rather than the temporal. The pain you face today will pale in the light of an eternity in heaven with God Almighty. Salvation is not earned; it is a gift from God. Suffering does nothing to "earn" heaven but you will receive a great reward for your pain for Christ's sake. Rather than rolling around in the pit of rejection and pain, Jesus tells you to keep your eyes on Him and on what is to come. Rejoice and leap for joy because your Savior knows what you are suffering for His sake and He will reward you for it – not just for a moment on earth but forever with Him in heaven.

Personal Touch:

Describe a time you have faced rejection because of your belief in Jesus Christ.

How can you keep this kind of rejection from undermining your joy and effectiveness for Christ?

Is the promise of eternity in heaven with God enough to get you through? Why or why not?

Prayer:

"Dear Heavenly Father, I praise your name and I praise you for sending your Son. I praise you when I suffer for your name's sake. I lift up my pain related to (insert an area where you are facing persecution) and I praise you for how you are using this for your glory and for my sanctification. May I become more like Christ through this experience. Help me to keep my eyes on eternity with you so that I may rejoice and leap for joy every day that you leave me on this earth. In the precious name of Jesus I pray, Amen."

Psalm 94:18-20
New International Version 1984 (NIV1984)

¹⁸ When I said, "My foot is slipping,"
your love, O LORD, supported me.
¹⁹ When anxiety was great within me,
your consolation brought joy to my soul.

Paraphrase this scripture (put it into your own words and try to include your name as if God were speaking directly to you):

Have you even been about to fall and knew it was coming? It is a slow-motion knowledge that the inevitable is coming. It is in those moments when there is no hope in self, in those around you, or even in the world that we can call out to and depend on our Lord. God's love is what holds us up when the terrain causes us to slip. God uses impossible situations, our weaknesses, and sometimes that inevitable moment you cannot avoid to show us His mercy and love. He allows us to experience that moment of having nothing to depend on but Him so that we will let go and experience His love wrapping around us and supporting us. Without these moments we will depend on our own power to cope and fail to see the precious hand of God holding us up.

When anxiety takes over and threatens to bring you down, when the wicked seem to be winning, God can give you joy. It is that open-handed letting go of everything and placing it in the trustworthy hands of our Heavenly Father that will give you the peace and happiness that defies the world. Even when it seems like the world is going to prevail, place your faith in the eternal judge who will have the final word. God's consolations, His love, His mercy, and His grace are the source of joy in your soul. And when you let all of that fear go, with a gasp and a cry, the weight will be lifted and it will be replaced with love and joy that is beyond description.

Personal Touch:

Have you ever experienced your proverbial foot slipping? What did it look like?

Did you reach out to God for help? Why or why not?

How might you handle future events like this differently and keep God's joy and peace throughout?

Prayer:

"Dear Heavenly Father, thank you for (list things in your life causing you to lose your footing) and how you are using this to draw me closer to you. I thank you that your love supports me and I ask that you will help me to trust your eternal vision for my life when it all seems so overwhelming. When my anxiety about (list your sources of anxiety) begins to take over, please remind me of your promises, your mercy, your grace and your faithfulness so that I may experience your joy within my soul. Allow the world around me to see this joy that defies circumstances and be drawn to you. I ask all these things in the name of Jesus my Savior, Amen."

1 Thessalonians 5:16-18
New International Version 1984 (NIV1984)

[16] Be joyful always; [17] pray continually; [18] give thanks in all circumstances, for this is God's will for you in Christ Jesus.

Paraphrase this scripture (put it into your own words and try to include your name as if God were speaking directly to you):

Here are three commands that are intimately tied together. The first is to be joyful always. Implicit here is that it IS possible to be joyful always. Think about that. It is possible to be joyful always! No matter what your situation, no matter what trial you face, no matter how hard life gets, it is possible to be joyful! This is spiritual joy that comes from gratitude for salvation and an understanding that everything, all comforts, and even our next breath, comes from our Father in Heaven.

Being joyful should, in turn, lead us to pray. If we are joyful always then we should be led to pray continually. The reverse is also true, that prayer leads us to God which then leads us to joy. Praying without ceasing does not mean that we should do nothing but pray. Rather, it means that nothing in this life should get in the way of our prayer. Each day should have quiet time of focused prayer that is a personal, intimate dialogue between you and your Father. Living a prayerful life is like having a constant open phone line to our Father – knowing that He is listening, adding regular comments directed toward Him, listening to God's directing, and at intervals through the day making requests and giving praise.

Being continually joyful and praying without ceasing will lead to giving thanks in all circumstances. God has a plan and will use every situation for His own purposes. Resting in the hands of our Father is a very humble and satisfying place to live. To know that God is using even our trials for His glory is a very relevant and thankful place to thrive.

Rejoicing, praying and being thankful no matter what your situation is God's will for you in Christ Jesus.

Personal Touch:

How can you be joyful always?

How do you allow life to get in the way of your prayer life? What positive changes will you make today?

Do others see you as being thankful in all circumstances? How can you increase gratitude in your life today?

Prayer:

"Dear Heavenly Father, I praise you that your will for me includes joy, prayer, and thankfulness. Be my constant guide toward rejoicing always. I thank you that this is even possible. Lead my prayer life. Help me to have an attitude of prayer throughout my day and to always have you at the forefront of my mind. May I have a thankful heart in all circumstances. When I find myself (include a circumstance that keeps you from a Godly attitude) help me to have a heart that is sensitive to the leading of the Holy Spirit. Guide me back to your will. In Jesus' name I pray, Amen."

Psalm 5:11
New International Version 1984 (NIV1984)

[11] But let all who take refuge in you be glad;
   let them ever sing for joy.
Spread your protection over them,
   that those who love your name may rejoice in you.

Paraphrase this scripture (put it into your own words and try to include your name as if God were speaking directly to you):

       This Psalm is a prayer of David. He is crying out to God for help during a time of great distress. In this verse, however, he shifts his focus to praying for others. David asks God to provide for others the same protection and joy that he so desperately needs for himself. He knows that God is a refuge and protection and that those who love God can sing for joy. This is joy stemming from love for the name, reputation, faithfulness and steadfastness of our Eternal Father. This is joy based on the reputation of God and never fails and is always available.

       When facing your own crisis, when staring down the barrel of pain and suffering, do you pray for others? What better balm for our own affliction than to become a servant of others, and for a moment to take our eyes off of ourselves and petition God on behalf of someone else. There is great joy in God our refuge, God our protection, and the name of God, but there is also great joy in praying for this very thing for others. What a blessing to hear a whole chorus singing for joy rather than just one lone voice.

Personal Touch:

How can you increase joy in your prayer life using David as an example?

How can you expand the focus of your prayer life today?

How has God been a refuge for you? Who can you pray for that needs God as a refuge right now?

Prayer:

"Dear Heavenly Father, I praise you for being my refuge and my protection. I love you and I trust and rest in your name. I lift up (include names of people in need) and ask that you spread your protection over them. Help them to love your name and all that it represents. Give them great rejoicing in you. Give them a song that can't be contained. Give them a song that flows forth and spreads your glory to all within their reach. Allow me to participate in this joyful singing and may our chorus of joy be pleasing to your ears. In the name of my Savior, Jesus, I pray, Amen."

Hebrews 12:2
New International Version 1984 (NIV1984)

[2] Let us fix our eyes on Jesus, the author and perfecter of our faith, who for the joy set before him endured the cross, scorning its shame, and sat down at the right hand of the throne of God.

Paraphrase this scripture (put it into your own words and try to include your name as if God were speaking directly to you):

As we go through our day we have our eyes (our focus) on something. Where are your eyes today? Are you focused on something other than Christ? Does your focus take you away from God or closer to Him? Here we are told to keep our eyes on Jesus as we walk through life on this earth. In all that we do and think, we are told to see life through the filter of Jesus. God gives us many things to fill our lives and we should enjoy them, work through them and use them for His glory. We are not to allow ourselves to be distracted from Him even with the busy lives we lead.

Jesus is the author and perfecter of our faith. He completed the work required to reconcile sinners to the perfect justice of God. He gave Himself as our sacrifice, not a simple, clean, easy sacrifice, but a sacrifice of great suffering, blood, and shame. Why did He do this for us? He did it for the joy. He suffered the anguish and humiliation because He knew that it would bring great joy to present the worst of sinners before His Father washed clean with His blood.

Our Savior experiences joy as He sits at the right hand of the throne of God. He is joyful when we see what He did, believe it, and focus our eyes on Him every moment of every day. What joy we can have knowing that Christ is rejoicing when we receive what He has freely given!

Personal Touch:

Where do you place most of your focus and attention throughout the day?

How does it change your thoughts about your own suffering when you think about how much Christ suffered for you?

How can you live a more God-focused life today?

Prayer:

"Dear Heavenly Father, I praise you for sending Jesus to be the author and perfecter of my faith. I praise you that I can keep my eyes focused on Him every moment to help me get through life in this fallen world. I lift up (insert something that draws your eyes away from Christ) to you and ask that you help me to see this through Jesus and that it would no longer be a distraction and a hindrance to my life in Christ. Help me to keep my eyes on you and may others see you shining through my submitted life. In the name of Jesus, the author and perfecter of my faith, Amen"

Psalm 92:4
New International Version 1984 (NIV1984)

⁴ For you make me glad by your deeds, O LORD;
I sing for joy at the works of your hands.

Paraphrase this scripture (put it into your own words and try to include your name as if God were speaking directly to you):

What has been your main focus in life lately? What place does praise and worship have? Is it reserved for church time alone? Praising God is how to live life. He alone is worthy of praise and the act of praising Him helps to keep our focus on God rather than on ourselves. This is a verse of praise. We are to praise Him as we look back on what God has done through eternity past, what He is doing in our present and looking forward to what He promises for our future.

It is impossible to comprehend the greatness of the works of God. We are incapable of truly understanding the depth and width of what God has done. Have you ever looked at the details of a flower? Looking closely reveals intricacies that boggle the mind. Not only is it beautiful but it is functional, and it participates in the plan of life for the whole earth. Why did God give us many kinds of flowers? He could have created a world with one kind of flower, or none. To understand the goodness of a God who would give us such beauty tied within the complexities of this functional world is astounding.

There are so many things that God has done and is doing for us every day. It is easy for sinful man to lose sight of the magnificence of the works of God's hands. It is easy because the picture of ourselves so often dominates our line of vision. Dropping that self-focus and looking at the works of God will make you glad. Not only will it make you glad, it will make you sing for joy!

Commit to making today the first day in a long line of God-focused days. Look for the deeds God has done and is doing in your life. See the works of His hands as you accomplish your tasks today. Sing for joy because God is mighty and He stoops down to be intimately related to you.

Personal Touch:

Look around and describe something you see that demonstrates the glory of your Heavenly Father.

How can taking your eyes off of yourself bring you greater joy?

How can you work toward this today?

Prayer:

"Dear Heavenly Father, forgive me for spending so much time and effort focusing on myself. Help me to have a God-focused day today. Reveal the work of your hands. Make me sensitive to your glory in what has seemed commonplace in the past. I cannot comprehend your greatness and I ask that you would help me to be vigilant in seeking it every day. When my focus us drawn to (<u>include something that gets in the way of praise</u>) help me to trust you with the outcome and keep my focus on your magnificence so that I might sing for joy today! In Jesus' name I pray, Amen."

1 Peter 1:3-9
New International Version 1984 (NIV1984)

[3] Praise be to the God and Father of our Lord Jesus Christ! In his great mercy he has given us new birth into a living hope through the resurrection of Jesus Christ from the dead, [4] and into an inheritance that can never perish, spoil or fade—kept in heaven for you, [5] who through faith are shielded by God's power until the coming of the salvation that is ready to be revealed in the last time. [6] In this you greatly rejoice, though now for a little while you may have had to suffer grief in all kinds of trials. [7] These have come so that your faith—of greater worth than gold, which perishes even though refined by fire—may be proved genuine and may result in praise, glory and honor when Jesus Christ is revealed. [8] Though you have not seen him, you love him; and even though you do not see him now, you believe in him and are filled with an inexpressible and glorious joy, [9] for you are receiving the goal of your faith, the salvation of your souls.

Paraphrase this scripture (put it into your own words and try to include your name as if God were speaking directly to you):

We have little in this world to rejoice over. What isn't leading us toward sin is simply perishing and ultimately leaving us wanting. Our treasure is laid up for us in heaven. Our inheritance in heaven will never perish, spoil or fade and it is being kept for us. In this we greatly rejoice! It can never be taken away from us or tarnish in any way. God has prepared for our eternity with Him.

He has also prepared for our temporal existence. We are shielded by God's power until that time. Oh, we will suffer grief and trials but not without hope or purpose as unbelievers do. Our suffering has intention - God does not desire that we experience pain but He uses it for His glory when we do. When gold is put through fire it is refined and the impurities are removed. Our trials show us our heart, and when brought through the fire we are increasingly sanctified and Christ within us is more clearly revealed to the world.

For those who believe in Christ our Savior, there is inexpressible and glorious joy in spite of the refining fire we will endure. Knowing how the story ends, with God victorious over evil and the release of our souls from the wickedness of our flesh, gives believers reason for rejoicing. May you have inexpressible and glorious joy today because you are receiving the goal of your faith, the salvation of your soul and knowing that God has a purpose for your life – to bring Him glory!

Personal Touch:

Where is your treasure? Would others agree with you?

How are you currently being refined for God's glory?

How does it change you to know that God has a purpose for your suffering?

Prayer:

"Dear Heavenly Father, I rejoice in your salvation and I praise you for the inheritance you are keeping for me in heaven. I know that the suffering I am enduring (include a trial you are dealing with) is a refining fire and I pray that you will use this moment to draw me closer to you. Give me your strength to persevere and help me to remember that you will use this for your glory. Use me, Lord. In Jesus' precious name I pray, Amen."

Proverbs 10:28
New International Version 1984 (NIV1984)

28 The prospect of the righteous is joy,
  but the hopes of the wicked come to nothing.

Paraphrase this scripture (put it into your own words and try to include your name as if God were speaking directly to you):

What are your hopes? Where do your expectations lie? For the wicked, their hope lies in their earthly desires. They may believe that there is a blissful eternity waiting for them, but this desire is based on nothing of substance. Whether you live your life in the now (attempting to create your own selfish heaven on earth) or you place your faith in something other than truth, your expectation for eternity will come to nothing. What does it profit a man to gain the whole world but lose his soul?

The hopes of the righteous bring joy! Placing your faith in the truth of the God of the Bible will not only bring fullness to the days of your life on earth, but an eternity of joy! There will be satisfaction for those whose hope is in the Lord. The wicked will be left empty here in this life. Seeking to fill themselves with the very best that the world has to offer will ultimately leave them wanting. The righteous do not place their hope in what is before them but in what is unseen and what is to come. Their hope will lead them into eternal joy!

So what do you place your hope in? Where does your faith rest? You either have to be perfectly righteous in your own right (good luck) or you must accept the righteousness of Christ. Rest in the joy that is yours through the gift of our Savior. Then your prospect is joy!

Personal Touch:

In what do you place your hope?

Do you truly live as if you believed God's promises?

How would living out a belief in God's promises change your life?

Prayer:

"Dear Heavenly Father, thank you that my prospect is joy. May my life be a light that draws unbelievers toward you and your salvation. I specifically pray for (include someone you know that needs God's salvation) and I ask that you would open their eyes and reveal yourself to them. Bring them to repentance and salvation so that they might have your joy. Thank you for giving me a hope that is sure. In Jesus' name I pray, Amen."

1 John 1:3-4
New International Version 1984 (NIV1984)

³ We proclaim to you what we have seen and heard, so that you also may have fellowship with us. And our fellowship is with the Father and with his Son, Jesus Christ. ⁴ We write this to make our joy complete.

Paraphrase this scripture (put it into your own words and try to include your name as if God were speaking directly to you):

The Apostles proclaim what they saw, heard and even touched regarding the life, death and resurrection of Jesus Christ. They do this so that they might have communion with other believers. Their fellowship with the Father and with Jesus Christ is so sufficient that they desire to share this intimacy with their brothers and sisters in Christ. Their joy is complete when they can meld their experiences with God into their lives with their friends.

Having a deep and personal relationship with the Father, Son, and Holy Spirit is vital to your spiritual livelihood. Having a deep and personal relationship with friends through the Father, Son, and Holy Spirit is the joyful icing on the cake. It may seem frivolous to seek friendships as a means to grow spiritually, but this is a fellowship that can draw you even closer to God.

Our creator designed us to be social beings. It was good for Adam to have Eve. There are seasons we endure where God removes people from us in order to draw us closer to Him. If you are in such a season praise God for the plans He has for you but never cease praying for and reaching out to others so that you can experience God's fellowship through other believers.

Personal Touch:

How lively is your spiritual life?

How might you improve your spiritual life today?

How does your relationship with God affect your relationships with others?

Prayer:

"Dear Heavenly Father, thank you for the plans you have for me, whether I am in a season blessed with people I can fellowship together with, or whether you desire my full attention to be on you. Thank you that I can experience spiritual intimacy with others through my relationship with you. I pray that you would help me to keep my relationship with you as the priority, and that I would see my relationships with others as perks. I thank you for (include someone you fellowship with). I lift them up and ask that you would use our relationship to bring glory to yourself. Help me to proclaim the truth that I have seen and heard so that others would be drawn to you. In Jesus' name I pray, Amen"

Psalm 95:1-3
New International Version 1984 (NIV1984)

[1] Come, let us sing for joy to the LORD;
  let us shout aloud to the Rock of our salvation.
[2] Let us come before him with thanksgiving
  and extol him with music and song.
[3] For the LORD is the great God,
  the great King above all gods.

Paraphrase this scripture (put it into your own words and try to include your name as if God were speaking directly to you):

It is our duty to praise God. Here is a description of what that duty looks like. Our praise is to be joyful. Holy joy is the basis of true praise. Our spirit is to lift our praise toward heaven with joyful singing. We are to be so overcome with God's holiness, goodness and with His provision of salvation that we shout with joy in music and song.

But what if we don't feel this joyful? What if we don't feel like lifting thanksgiving and songs to heaven? Where does this joy come from? It comes from God himself. God does not ask us to rely on our own fleeting emotions to create this kind of worship. God, in His great wisdom and kindness, provides joy for us through the Holy Spirit, our helper. The fruit of the Spirit is produced through a life that is submitted to God and a life that is available to be used by Him. When it comes to joy, God will provide you with joy. He then desires you to give that joy back to Him in worship. As always, God does not leave us to struggle along on our own. He will provide.

The obedience of praise and worship (even when the "emotion" is not there) will bring you to Godly joy and peace. Do what you know God is asking you to do, and He is faithful to provide that which you are lacking. He can do this because He is the great God, the great King above all gods. We praise Him not because we "feel", we "feel" because we praise.

Personal Touch:

What does your praise life look like?

How would your life look if you lived it completely submitted to God?

How does submission to God lead you to praise?

Prayer:

"Dear Heavenly Father, I praise you and I adore you. Thank you for being my Rock of salvation. Thank you that you are the great King above all gods. Lord, I thank you specifically for (include something God has recently blessed you with). Help me to keep my life focused on worshipping you and you alone. Don't let anything become more important than my relationship with you. And for those times when I don't feel your joy, Lord, I pray that you would help me to submit and be available to be used by the Holy Spirit for your mighty work. During times of grief and suffering, help me to praise you for what you are going to do in and through my life. May I find peace, trust and spiritual joy from your presence. In Jesus' Holy name I pray, Amen."

Jude 1:24-25
New International Version 1984 (NIV1984)

[24] To him who is able to keep you from falling and to present you before his glorious presence without fault and with great joy— [25] to the only God our Savior be glory, majesty, power and authority, through Jesus Christ our Lord, before all ages, now and forevermore! Amen.

Paraphrase this scripture (put it into your own words and try to include your name as if God were speaking directly to you):

It is easy to get bogged down in our sin and in our failures. It seems that the closer our walk with God becomes, the more sin we see in ourselves. The more we grow in Christ, the more repulsive our sinful nature becomes. While we must confess our sins, we are not to live our lives as slaves to sin but as slaves to Christ. God is able to keep us from falling, and we will enter the very presence of God's glory, faultless and washed clean by the blood of Christ. Not only does this give us great joy it gives God great joy!

Jesus is the creator and completer. He is able to accomplish our ultimate sanctification in heaven, and where there is holiness there is joy. When we find ourselves in the very presence of God in heaven, our hearts will experience a joy that has no equal on earth. For now, we have Christ within us, allowing us to tap into that joy as an advance on what we will experience in glory.

Personal Touch:

Would you describe yourself as a slave to sin or a slave to Christ?

How can you increase your time as a slave to Christ rather than a slave to sin?

How do you tap into the joy of your future with Christ while you still struggle here on earth?

Prayer:

"Dear Heavenly Father, thank you that you are able to keep me from falling. Thank you that I will be brought into your presence, faultless and clean because of the sacrifice of your Son. Thank you that there will be great joy in that moment! Let my eyes remain fixed on you rather than myself so that I may experience the joy that is found in your holiness. I pray this to the only God, our Savior, who is the embodiment of glory, majesty, power and authority, through Jesus Christ our Lord, before all ages, now and forevermore! Amen."

Psalm 97:10-12
New International Version 1984 (NIV1984)

10 Let those who love the LORD hate evil,
for he guards the lives of his faithful ones
and delivers them from the hand of the wicked.
11 Light is shed upon the righteous
and joy on the upright in heart.
12 Rejoice in the LORD, you who are righteous,
and praise his holy name.

Paraphrase this scripture (put it into your own words and try to include your name as if God were speaking directly to you):

Do you ever wonder if God has a plan for your life? The very fact that you are still in the land of the living is proof that God still has a plan for your life. The Lord guards the lives of His people, and we are here on this earth to fulfill His purposes. But larger than this plan for our life is the plan for our eternity. Our Lord guards our souls. Not one of His sheep will be lost – not one. He knows His flock and He does not leave us alone to walk in the dark.

God's light is sown in the righteous. We are given the very righteousness of Christ. His light is planted within us like seeds of joy. Believers are told to expect suffering, so these seeds of joy may lie beneath the dirt of tribulation. Whether we feel it or not, the joy is there because Christ is there and He desires the seeds of joy to grow into strong trees of rejoicing. All joy leads to and stems from God.

Our rejoicing is in the Lord and in His holiness. Even the angels call Him "Holy, Holy, Holy" in their exultation. God's holiness demands praise, glory and honor. But it also calls for thanksgiving because through grace we are partakers of His holiness. The lost quake in the light of His holiness, but the saints rejoice in His holy name as they remember what He has given for them.

Seek your Holy Father today. Feel the warmth of His light as it shines down upon you. Allow His holiness to embolden the seeds of joy to take root in your heart. Don't let life distract you from your purpose. God has you here for a reason. Let His light reveal your path and your joy.

Personal Touch:

Have you experienced the warmth and light of God? Describe what happened.

How do you increase your time spent living in God's warmth and light?

How can you rejoice in the Lord today?

Prayer:

"Dear Heavenly Father, I stand amazed at your holiness. I am humbled that through your grace you have given me the very righteousness of Christ. I pray that you would help me to reflect your holiness to the world and not allow the darkness of sin to cover your light. Sometimes I don't feel your joy. Sometimes I allow (include something that steals your joy) to rob me of the joy you desire me to experience. I pray that you would teach me to give that over to you and trust in your sovereign plan for my life and for my eternity. May I never forget that you will never forget or forsake me! May my tree of joy be planted by streams of living water. In Jesus' holy name I pray, Amen."

Romans 15:13
New International Version 1984 (NIV1984)

[13] May the God of hope fill you with all joy and peace as you trust in him, so that you may overflow with hope by the power of the Holy Spirit.

Paraphrase this scripture (put it into your own words and try to include your name as if God were speaking directly to you):

Here we have a prayer that Paul prayed for each of us. He desires that the God of hope will fill us with all joy and peace. First, take a moment to park on the title given God – the God of hope. Our faith can be strengthened by seeing God in this light. And this hope is an expectation of good, not just a hope based on undependable, sinful men.

This God of hope can fill us. How often have you felt emptiness in your very soul that needs filling? We can pour vast quantities of earthly vanity into that hole but it is God who fills us to overflowing. He fills us with all joy and peace. Notice that it is not some joy and peace. He fills us with all kinds of joy and peace as we trust in Him. Trust Him enough to let go, to fall into His loving arms and allow Him to fill you to overflowing. It is the power of the Holy Spirit – the very power that raised Christ Jesus from the dead - that causes you to be inundated with hope that will satiate your hunger. You will be filled with joy and peace that is the very fruit of the Holy Spirit. This joy and peace doesn't just fill you, it flows forth from you.

Personal Touch:

What would your life look like if you lived every moment believing that God is the God of hope?

What have you poured into yourself in an attempt to fill that empty space inside? Did it fulfill you?

How can you live out your trust in God today?

Prayer:

"Dear Heavenly Father, thank you for loving me so much that you desire me to be filled to overflowing with your hope, joy and peace. I ask now that you, my God of hope, would fill me with all joy and peace. I pray that you would help me to trust you with (include something keeping you from peace) and that you would help me to let it go into your steadfast arms. I pray that your Holy Spirit would be free to pour forth your fruit from my life into the lives of others who need it. Thank you for loving me this much. In Jesus' name I pray, Amen."